The Engaging Leader

Shlomit Weiss

Producer & International Distributor
eBookPro Publishing
www.ebook-pro.com

The Engaging Leader
Shlomit Weiss

All cases are as the author see it and there is no connection between the names in the book and real people

Translation: Tamar Landau

Contact: shlomit-weiss@hotmail.com
ISBN: 9798780747215

THE
ENGAGING
LEADER

HOW LEADERS WHO CARE
ACHIEVE OUTSTANDING BUSINESS RESULTS

SHLOMIT WEISS

CONTENTS

This book was made possible thanks to all the unique and wonderful people I've worked with over the years. With you, I have learned, grown, developed as a manager and a leader, and created my unique leadership methods.

A special thanks to my mother, who was a motivating power and always inspired me with the faith to write this book. Throughout my career, she supported me, saying: "Remember that you are good, knowing and capable." For this, I thank her wholeheartedly.

INTRODUCTION

Birthday

September 22, my birthday. I was standing, excited, in the front row of a huge convention hall in San Francisco. I was surrounded by 5,000 people, who were applauding the project I had managed that had just premiered. I could not believe all this was happening. I was proud of the success of my team; I was happy and thrilled with the support we'd received. After a few years of strained work, I felt exhilarated: We were making a global impact! Without a doubt, this was the most special gift I could have received for my birthday.

That same evening, after the exciting day was over, and people congratulated me everywhere, my mother called. "Happy birthday!" she said, "May you always succeed and be happy and satisfied."

"Thanks, Mom. Today was full of congratulations and successes; the project was a great success, and I was so thrilled!"

"Good, Shlomiti; I am very pleased to hear that. Keep it up."

"Thanks, Mom," I answered. Through all the joy and excitement, a tough question came to my mind. "Mom, what do you think Dad would say?" I will never know the answer; but I do know, without a doubt, that the sudden loss of my father when I was a young child significantly influenced the person I grew up to be. My warm and supportive home, which remained so despite the loss, made me behave, lead and work with my heart, and not just with my head.

Tu Bishvat Eve, I was eleven years old. We were waiting for Mom and Dad to return from work and take us to the circus. It was supposed to be my first time at the circus, and I was really looking forward to it. Mom and Dad never showed up, and it was getting late. I went to the window in the corner room, where I had a view of the entire street, so that I could see them as soon as they arrived. Time went by; it was getting late, but there was no sign of Mom and Dad. Obviously, it was too late to go to the circus; but at that moment, we only wanted Mom and Dad to get home. I was pacing back and forth, from the window to the living room, anticipating my parents' return. There was no sign of them.

Mom came home very late with some people from work. Dad was not with them. She entered the living room quietly, hugged us and sat us both beside her on the sofa. Then she said, "Dad is gone; he passed away." Shocked, I looked at my sister, and then at my mother, understanding nothing. Mom did not cry; she just hugged us quietly. I wanted to cry, but I did not want to make her sad, so I quietly went to my room – to the same corner window – and cried there. Mom said we should go to sleep, because we would have a harsh day ahead of us the next day. All night long, I dreamed that this was a mistake, that something had been wrong, that it was impossible that my father would never return ....

The next day, we held the funeral. Many people surrounded us, everybody taking care of us, and I did not know what to do. I left the building and saw a few girls from school gazing at me from around the corner. I was ashamed. I wanted to be like them; I did not want to be different; I did not want to be pitied.

That day changed my life. I busied myself with being just like everybody else, showing people that they should not pity me, that I was not miserable. I wanted to succeed in everything that I was doing, to do the best I could – with no help – without bothering Mom, who was always working hard, making sure that we would have all we need. I wanted to do well, to make Mom and my family happy, to get the best grades, to help around the house, to have a positive point of view and to never complain or ask for help. This was so strong an impulse and is still embedded in me to this very day. It shaped the person I became—the way I do things. I always get along at work; I do everything in the best way possible; I excel; and I always see the positive, in any situation. My mother was always supportive and made sure that we would be alright and short of nothing. From this atmosphere of warmth and love, I also learned to give with all my heart, with plenty of sensitivity and caring, in any situation.

Too Sensitive

"You are too sensitive; you will never succeed to grow as a manager," my boss told me during a personal meeting session for the annual employee evaluation. This conversation ended my first year as a manager. Tears came rolling down my cheeks, and I could not utter a single word. "There was good progress made at work, and the results are good," my boss continued his feedback, but I could not listen to what he was saying. My mind was racing: What did it mean? Would I have to change course? It really hurt my feelings. This is horrible, I thought; I love managing; I had built a good group with a nice work environment, a group that achieves results—so why should I stop managing now?

"Look, it's not that bad," my boss continued. "I am not saying you didn't do a good job now; but in the future, it will be difficult for you to be promoted to senior management," he tried to calm my tears. In a daze, I heard only half sentences. I was deeply insulted (the truth is, I am sensitive ...), but I also tried to reason, to not cry, to not show that I was offended. I felt I had to show him that everything was fine, that I would improve and move on; but honestly, my tears kept rolling uncontrollably down my cheeks. "It was a good year, all in all, and the team was well-built and met all the tasks on schedule," my boss summarized his feedback. "Best of luck," he said and left the office.

I stayed in the office on my own, trying to digest everything, to understand it and to calm myself down. I summarized the year for myself briefly: I work with my heart and my soul; I give plenty of attention to people, creating a good environment for the group; my employees help each other and enjoy working with one another. I demand high-quality results from my employees, insisting they submit their work on schedule, be professional and plan everything to the finest detail. Some people are afraid of me and prepare for a long time before coming to show me their plans, as everyone knows I set a very high standard in all my work. All these factors helped me succeed and get good results. But I had just heard that I was too sensitive, and that I would not make it as a higher manager, even though this is the work I want to keep doing. I decided to do the best that I can, to continue to act as I see fit and to prove that I can make it.

A few years later, I was serving in the United States; and, as many employees were leaving the group in Israel, one of the senior managers called me and said, "Shlomit, we really need you to return; we need a manager that will work from their soul to build and to manage a strong and engaged team."

Today, I serve as a senior vice president at Intel, following terms as senior vice president at Mellanox and, earlier, as vice president at Intel, and having the experience of quite a few senior and complex management positions. Truthfully, my sensitivity became a great advantage in my work and part of my success in the senior management of large and complex organizations. The combination of professionalism, uncompromised results and endless sensitivity might sound strange, but it played a critical and central part in my successes in management and in leading grand, complex projects.

In this book, I present examples from my own experience in management and leadership, including conclusions about the way to deal with various situations by implementing an array of techniques. I discuss leadership, professionalism, values and – at the same time – honest concern for people and their multifaceted usefulness, which enables the achievement of excellent results.

1

DIFFERENT BEGINNINGS

Every manager knows that when you start managing a new group, it is customary to conduct a few processes: initial acquaintance-ship, organizational structuring and defining strategies, objectives and courses of action. Obviously, these are all important processes; but, in my opinion, the most important thing is to modify the be-ginning – the acquaintanceship, the method of defining objectives and all initial steps – to the specific group—to the people them-selves and to the types of challenges confronting them. True—this is the beginning; you are not familiar with the group; sometimes, the group members are even unfamiliar with one another; but I believe adjusting the beginning is possible using the following means: First, the most important characteristics and issues are visible from day one; and they can be recognized in an extremely short time. Second, you should be open to change and to adapting your method of action as you go. Third, you should work from your soul, observing every individual separately, in depth and not just on the surface. Here are some examples of different beginnings:

First Relocation Far from Home

I managed the Cache Group for three years, until the company decided to pivot and stop development in my area. When I first heard of this decision, I was shocked. This had been my area of expertise from the moment I had come to the company; we had a group of wonderful people, performing good projects in an excellent environment. What would happen to the entire team now?

Once I realized that this decision was final, I started to look for jobs for my entire group. I decided to find a meaningful role for every one of them, a role in which they would be satisfied and appreciated. I held endless negotiations with different executives in the company in various positions, and with my employees, until I knew for sure that everybody was satisfied with their new placements. They were laughing at me and referring to me as "Mother Goose" taking care of her goslings.

When all this was over, I had to confront the dilemma about my role. I had no idea what I was going to do. One of those days, as I was still looking around, the site manager called me and asked, "How do you feel about going to work in the States?"

Many employees in the company were yearning for a job abroad and even had asked for one specifically, but I had never thought of it—up to that moment. I was really surprised at the offer, and I only answered, wondering, "I don't know. Why abroad?"

"This is a good chance to get to know other groups," the manager said, "a more complex project, other work methods."

"I have to think about it," I said. "I don't know if it suits me."

"I suggest you fly over there for a few days and see if there is any role you want, any role that suits you, and then we can talk."

"Yeah, fine; good idea."

More than I was afraid of the role itself, I was worried about the travel and life elsewhere for a few years. On the one hand, I was alone, with no children; on the other hand, I was tied to my little family, to my mother and my sister. They were always there to celebrate with on holidays, to consult with during major events. How would I manage far away and alone? This was frightening.

I decided to go for one week to look at possible jobs and then to make up my mind. Deep down, I was certain they would never offer me anything real and that this would render the decision irrelevant. But reality was different than I imagined. I received two offers for highly interesting jobs, with an option to be promoted and to grow as a manager. I returned home, even more perplexed than when I had left, as I was handling an even larger conflict. I had been offered a good and interesting position, but I was scared to live alone in a foreign country. I decided to be open and talk to my boss about it. Openness and heart-to-heart conversations, including up the hierarchy (and not only with peers or subordinates), allow for better connections and more creative solutions for any problem. In retrospect, this conversation would allow me to make my decision and would open many doors in my career.

I returned to meet with my boss and to decide how to continue my professional path.

"How was it?" he asked, "What do you say?"

"There is a role that seems interesting," I answered, "but I am truly afraid of this for a whole other reason. I think it's terrifying to live alone in a foreign country I'm not familiar with."

"I see; that can be really complicated. This could be a great opportunity to advance your career, but it's your call—you do what you think is right," my boss concluded the discussion.

I deliberated about it for a few more days, and then I had an idea that calmed my anxiety. I met with my boss to suggest it.

"I would like to take this job, but I am asking that you allow me to return at any time, even before the end of the period, if things don't turn out right, and if I don't get along there. Is it possible?"

"Fine by me," my boss answered, "but let me check with the project manager there, as he is the one that has to agree to it. I will get back to you as soon as I have an answer."

A few days later, my boss called me and said, "I checked with the project manager abroad; he wants you on board and agreed that you could come, and if you are dissatisfied, that you can return before the end of your term" (usually a job abroad is for a term of two years).

As far as I was concerned, this was an excellent answer. On the one hand, I was receiving an opportunity and a very interesting position, and on the other, my fear was not as big, because I knew I could return if I didn't make it there.

All the bureaucracy, forms and living arrangements began. I am a practical person, and I prepared everything well and was ready to go, but my heart was afraid of many things. How would I get to know other people? What would happen during the holidays? I was used to being with my family on holidays. And if I needed help, who should I turn to? I suppressed these thoughts, even without good answers, and kept on preparing.

Moving day arrived. After saying goodbye to my entire family, my mom came with me to the airport, and we parted with plenty of hugs, kisses and "good lucks."

As I sat down in the plane on my own, for a brief moment I thought: What did I do?! What is this nonsense?! But I immediately balanced these thoughts with my enthusiasm for the new job and the great opportunity, and having calmed myself, began thinking that everything would turn out for the good.

When I landed, all the initial arrangements had been done as well as possible, by a relocation employee who knew the procedures and bureaucracy helping with anything needed. In the first week, in order to get to know others, I met a few Israeli families; they "adopted" me, took me on trips and invited me to dinners to make me feel comfortable.

At work, the beginning was not simple. I was working at the same company and was told that here would have the same culture, that everything would be the same and that things would be easy; but to be honest, work was completely different, from small things to bigger things.

I started out managing a small group called LOC, which oversaw planning one of the main functional units of the project. In my work in Israel, I was used to walking the cubicles every morning, asking how things were, sensing the mood and the motivation of the group, and creating an open, pleasant atmosphere. For the new group that did not know me, this was strange, and everyone took it differently. I paid attention to the various employee reactions in order to understand how they felt and to adjust myself to them. I was the same person, but I always adapted my management style to the person with whom I was working.

With one of the employees, who was fresh out of college when he had joined the team, the difference was extraordinary.

"Good morning, Razah, how are you?" I asked.

Razah stood in front of me and answered: "I managed to do this, but I did not finish that yet; today, I will do this and that, and I will be done with it, for sure."

Each time I asked him how he was, he related only to work, in a stressed-out, panicked manner. This was not my intention at all. I wanted to create a pleasant atmosphere, and his reaction was the complete opposite. I decided not to stress him out and kept on checking on the other group members. I always skipped his cubicle.

A few weeks later – when I felt he was calmer – I innocently asked him, when it was just the two of us: "Do you know why I came to your office every morning?"

"Yes," he answered, "to know how work was doing."

"Not at all. I just wanted to see how you were, to wish you a good morning, nothing else. When I want to know how work is doing, I will ask you directly; I am not embarrassed to," I said and laughed to ease things. I recognized a sudden relief in his face, and he laughed, saying nothing.

Since that day, I visited him in the mornings again; and he was relaxed, remained seated and told me about things that had happened to him in the past day.

I adjusted; I was open and direct, and achieved the open, pleasant atmosphere I desired that is so important to cooperation.

In a short while, the entire team became used to this custom, and even when I was not there, they got used to chatting with one another during the first few minutes of the workday. This was a small change, but later, it served as an important factor for our cooperation, especially during the stressful stages of the project.

My efforts to build a team whose members helped and supported one another lasted through time and spread in all directions. After about six months, I decided to hold a gathering at my house for all the team members and their spouses. During the team meeting, I announced: "This Saturday, you and your spouses are invited to my place for an Israeli dinner." For the first moment, they fell quiet; then they thanked me politely. Suddenly someone asked, wondering: "With our spouses? This is interesting; we have never met our colleagues' spouses, and we have been working together for a few years." Finally, the wonder – and perhaps the embarrassment – subsided. Everyone came to the gathering; the evening was great fun, and it strengthened the relationships between the employees and with the entire group, which was very helpful for a few difficulties and stressful tasks.

The bond of the group was so strong that, even after my return to Israel, we kept in touch, and whenever I was in the States, we would hold a "team meeting," even though each of them already belonged to another group, or another company altogether.

The attention given to each person and his reactions is extremely important and should always be taken into account for adapting the way in which you regard him. I had a clear aim, to be open and to initiate a good atmosphere with everyone, but in Razah's case, my behavior created the exact opposite effect—stress and discomfort. The attention I had given him, and the fact I had recognized its effect in a timely fashion and changed my behavior, allowed me to get the desired result.

Sensitivity to the environment, and to the intentions and objectives of everyone, enables the creation of a genuine connection and makes every individual feel he is important and understood—and this is a highly important objective.

Getting to Know Your Employees Up Close

When I was sent on another mission in the States, it was an easier decision to make, and the move was simpler. I was invited to manage a project with a group in Folsom, California. I viewed this position as an opportunity for progress and development. I was already experienced in working overseas, and I decided quickly that I wanted to take the opportunity.

About two weeks before the project started, I took a flight to Folsom to meet with the entire group—about two hundred people. During this meeting, my boss, Raffi, had intended to inform the group that their former boss, Mike, was leaving, and that I was stepping into his place. I had met Mike, and he'd filled me in about the group, its goals and assignments. The next day, I went with Mike and Raffi to meet the group.

Raffi started the meeting: "I want to let you know that Mike decided to transfer to another job here in Folsom, and that Shlomit came from Israel to take his place and manage the group."

For the first moment, the room fell into complete silence, and Raffi continued: "Shlomit has experience in the design, architecture and the management of various groups. Within a few weeks, she will move to Folsom and be here for the entire duration of her job." When Raffi finished his speech, he invited the group members to ask questions: "If you have any questions for Shlomit, Mike or me, you are welcome to ask them." I moved to the center of the room, looking around at all the people, looking at Raffi, not knowing what to expect. After a few seconds of silence, someone raised her hand and asked: "Shlomit, what do you bring to the group that will enable you to solve all its problems?" I had no idea what she was talking about. Which problems was the group experiencing? I had not started the job yet; I did not know what to expect, and people were already asking me what I was bringing to the table? The lady continued to ask: "Raffi, why do we have to bring a manager from

Israel and don't take someone local, from our group?"

I thought this might save me and that Raffi would answer the question, but he politely said, "I will let Shlomit answer that." That was it; I had no choice and no more time to think. I started to answer, "I need to get to know the group, to see its strengths and its areas to improve or change. From what I learn, together with you and with the management team in the group, we can achieve success for the group and the entire company. My objective is to present to the company the required outputs, while creating and strengthening the group." I felt satisfied with myself; I had gotten away with this complicated question and thought that the following questions would be directed to Raffi and Mike—and then came the following question: "You are from Israel, so how can we know that you will care about the group in Folsom?"

This was another challenging question – although slightly less than the previous one, I thought – and answered immediately: "I am going to live in Folsom for the next couple of years—so this is my place, and I will obviously look out for the success of this team."

By the end of the meeting, a few other questions were asked, but luckily some were directed to Mike and Raffi. I relaxed, but I realized that I was facing a challenging task. The team was not so happy to see me as their manager—to put things mildly. I immediately began planning how to start—planning how I would be able to connect with the group and understand the background to their questions. It was obvious that getting acquainted with these people, getting close to them, understanding what went on in the

THE ENGAGING LEADER | 25

group, and expressing warmth and care – side by side with the direct, informational approach – would be key here.

As I entered my role, I held plenty of conversations with the employees and the managers. I listened to what was said, but I asked every one of them two additional questions: First—"what do you think should be the first thing I should work on in the group?" This question allowed me to learn and focus on the problems – the things they would like to change, the things they consider to be disrupting success – but it also allowed me to get closer to them and to demonstrate my openness to listen and learn from them. This is a highly important factor when coming to a new group and a new place you know nothing about. Second, the question I always end with—"What is working well in the group? What do you like the most here?" Most people stopped and were surprised by this question—especially after they had been so enthused about what was wrong and what needed to be changed. I did not let go; I waited encouragingly until I got an answer, and everyone came up with an answer. This question is extremely important, because it allows one to learn the good and successful things; and, most importantly, it allows ending the discussion with something positive and optimistic for the person I am talking to. I strongly believe that work should be fun, at least most of it, and that it is always better to find a positive aspect of it. For this reason, it is important for me to end such a conversation in a positive and optimistic manner and to enable this optimistic thinking for everyone.

I did not come to the group with big declarations, but in every conversation that presented a problem, I provided a small practical offer about what could be done, how we could think differently and why now it would work out. In some cases, I even clearly stated that I was not sure what needed to be done and that I would think about it, because I had to learn the situation in depth and figure it out to find a solution.

One of the major problems was the lack of trust and support between the managers in the group. Each of them told me how the others were wrong. In each conversation, I was careful not to take sides. I always concentrated on the individual I was talking to, advising him on how to be more successful and to work more satisfactorily, and disregarding the arguments about others. It is not always easy to avoid being biased or judgmental, but it is highly important as a manager, so that the disagreements between other people will not get worse.

As is often done when creating a management team, we scheduled a day in which we would discuss the organization's objectives, common goals, etc. This time, I wanted a personal atmosphere that would yield an experience – that would enable people to be open, to cooperate and to feel at ease – and that was the reason I decided to hold this day at my house. We opened with a little getting-to-know-you game and got to work. With an emphasis on cooperation, we conducted an exercise in which each of us shared something meaningful from his world (not necessarily related to work), that defined the way he manages and that shaped him as a leader. This is not a simple exercise, especially in a group whose members have so many tensions and such great competition; and I opened and introduced myself first. I told them how I grew up with only my mother, and how it taught me to do everything alone, because my mother was busy and I did not wish to interrupt her. I shared how, in the IDF, I initially did not get accepted to the officers' course, but that, later, they decided to give me a chance and that this made me do my best—to show gratitude for the opportunity. The room fell silent, and everyone was paying attention to me. I talked about personal things they did not know; I talked about professional successes and failures. Without a doubt, I was personal with them. After I was done, I gave them time to work on their own and think for a while before they introduced themselves. After about fifteen minutes, they started to introduce themselves; and I noticed how attentive the people were, how surprised they were, how amazed and often compassionate they were. Even though these people had worked together for many years, a new attribute was opened up in everyone, and it created an atmosphere of receptiveness and openness. After a short coffee break, the terms were right to discuss cooperation and mutual assistance, and the discussion went great. Later that day, we held strategy talks about the organization, as well as friendly conversation—all in good spirits. Without a doubt, this day was the most important day, and it redefined the expectations from the management team.

Obviously not everything works out great after a single day; but that day set a new direction, expectations, a common language, methods of action. Such a concentrated day allows us later to make demands and corrections—and not to accept incorrect behaviors.

I managed this group for two years, and throughout that time, I emphasized openness, authenticity, caring for others, morality and integrity; and refused complaints, whining and talk about other people. With all my openness and desire to understand and get to know others, it was highly important to maintain high demands and quality results, and to define my exact expectations of others. The focus of working on this team was to improve the relationships between the employees, but such relationships are built better when there are great challenges alongside high expectations and uncompromised professionalism.

Two years later, the project ended and was wrapped up. The team worked with a great deal of cooperation. By the way, some managers who did not get along left along the way; but this only made the organization better and made the employees who did stay there more focused, desiring success. Even though there are employees who freak out when a manager leaves, I don't think it's too bad, especially if they leave because they do not get along with the group or disagree with the direction the group is heading in.

At my farewell party, one of the employees summarized briefly: "What you had for us was evident, and you have contributed greatly to the team's success. Thank you very much and best of luck."

I have presented two examples of my beginnings in new groups, which were – without a doubt – extremely different from each other. The commonality was that in each beginning – as the leader

– I had to learn about, become familiar with and get to know the group and its members. This is the basis for defining the method of action – the way by which we go about harnessing the management and the group for tasks – to achieve the best results for the company. Familiarity and initial learning define our method of action and are the reason it will have differences and be suited to the group and its members. It is highly important to be flexible and to adapt the way you work in order to achieve your objectives. Your work methodology should always be an integration of tasks, objectives, dynamics and common work.

Every time you manage a new group, you go through definite stages and processes: You must always hold an introduction talk between attendees, set goals and objectives and define work plans. But when you do all these sensitively and with attention given to people and to details, when you look beyond the dry facts – beyond what is said directly – it allows for a deeper understanding of the dynamics within the group, the character of its members and the way to behave. Such deep understanding and acquaintance are possible when you are working with your emotions, when you analyze situations in a humane way and figure out solutions while taking the people who are supposed to do the tasks into account—and not only the task at hand. This method always leads to a higher level of engagement and cooperation by people with any task—including the most difficult ones. Considering the needs of people and the interpersonal dynamics is far more important when you want to change the group and the organizational structure.

Insights and Applications

- It is important that the manager adjusts to the person in front of him and to his needs. When you understand the person standing in front of you, you can use the most suitable method to succeed in connecting to him, which generates better results.

- Questions that allow for openness and trust: "What should I improve?" A question that testifies about openness, sharing and the desire to learn. "What works best in this group?" A question that allows ending the conversation on an optimistic, positive tone.

- True openness, direct conversations and role modeling make the individual in front of you open up and allow for a deeper mutual understanding. Getting your employees to know one another is the basis for building the team and for defining good goals and objectives. This approach is most effective when it is required to improve the relationships between managers or within the group itself.

2

A COLLABORATIVE MODEL FOR BUILDING
AN EFFECTIVE GROUP

Deep familiarity with people and a deep understanding of the organizational objectives are certainly important to creating a group or making big changes in an organization. In the real world, when making large changes, it is not always possible to prepare in advance; sometimes, it is required to create a new organization without proper time for real acquaintance. When you are in such a situation and you must build an organization, it is important to be effective and objective, doing it wisely. This task is extremely difficult, because most known methods are based on deep acquaintance with objectives and people. During one of the shifts in my career, I had to build a new organization and did not have the time to learn about it or to get to know the employees in advance. I developed a collaborative and efficient method I will lay out here, which allowed me to define an organizational structure in a short time, and created an effective, highly successful organization.

One day, I was appointed to manage the entire engineering department of the large server group. This was a big job for me. I had to create a group of more than 1,500 people, who formerly had worked in five different groups. Each of the groups used to report to a different manager and used to work according to different methods, and now it was decided to make the work more efficient by uniting these groups and making me the new manager. Without a doubt, this was a great honor. I was given an extremely heavy responsibility and was expected to produce rapid results, efficiency and the promotion of everybody's work methods.

My first task was to build the organization. It was obvious that the mere connection of the groups as they were would not lead to efficiency and the improvement of the work methods. It was required to unite missions, unite organizations, let them learn from each other, avoid duplicates and yet maintain the uniqueness and challenges of each group. What I had to do was obvious, but I knew that the groups themselves would be less fond of the change and would rather stay separate, as they were. Theoretically, I knew what was required; but I was unfamiliar with the groups, their managers, the advantages and disadvantages of each group, and what should be preserved or changed. You usually get to know the group, the people and the tasks on hand, and base your defining of the group structure on this knowledge. This was not the situation this time, and I was required to think in a different manner. While I was deliberating, I started to create a process that would help me reach my objective.

I was required to work with the current managers, to get to know the tasks and the groups through them. However, it was evident that not everyone who was currently a manager would remain so in the new organization. It was complicated to move people around; but change is necessary and makes work and the organizational structure more efficient. I strongly considered the extent to which I should share with the others, or whether to make decisions on my own, and – in any case – I knew that, eventually, not everyone would be fond of the change. I wanted to manage an effective process and to build the group correctly, according to the organizational objectives and targets, to correctly divide the roles. I defined the various stages I intended to go through and immediately started to implement them.

I chose the participants in the creation process, including all current managers of every group and their staff, and sent the following message to them: "Congratulations; you were chosen to be one of the key employees that define and create the new group. Your knowledge and expertise are critical for the creation of a successful organization. In about two weeks, we will meet face to face in Haifa Design Center for two concentrated days to define the new organization. It should be mentioned that not everybody who participates in this creation process will necessarily be part of my direct management team. Good luck to everyone on our shared creation; see you at the gathering; bring plenty of good ideas."

It was vital that I stress that not everyone selected would be senior managers in the new organization. I did not want to encourage any expectations that might later lead to great disappointment.

Before the meeting, each of them was required to prepare a presentation about his group. In the preparation instructions, I provided one structured part: the group objectives, its products, its size and its interfaces with other groups. In addition, everyone had to prepare a page or two about his group characteristics. This task was left open, to learn what important things the manager had to say about the group and to learn about the manager himself, about the way he presented and about things which were important to him. I always find that open-ended and less definite components are an excellent way to get to know more, to discover leadership and character, to create a deeper understanding of things and to learn how the individual manages and thinks.

Two weeks went by quickly. During this time, I was busy preparing two days of meetings—charting a good, clear process. I knew these were highly critical days for the success of the entire organization from that point on; and yet, I had never done such a process on my own, and I felt like I was inventing a new method, not knowing whether it would work.

Everybody arrived excited; they did not know what to expect or how things would be conducted; and some were very skeptical, as none of them had participated in such a process before. Usually, the leader defines the structure and informs the group about it, and now suddenly, we were attempting to complete such a task with a group of about twenty people. We were convened in a room, and the HR representative had joined me as she wanted to help, although she had never been part of such a process. She was also new to the group and did not know any of the managers.

"Good morning and welcome to two of the most important days for defining our organizational structure and the way in which we work—which will be key to the success of the organization," I opened the day and kept on talking. Everyone was paying attention and trying to understand what was going on and how it would work. "To reach mutual success, I ask and expect from each one of you to think about what is right for the entire organization; but try to detach, as much as possible, your personal role from the needs of the organization. I know that you are highly experienced and mature managers and that, despite all difficulties, you will be able to make such a detachment."

The room fell silent, no one reacted; everybody's faces showed that there were some who really understood and connected, and some who were not so clear on how such detachment could be done.

I chose not to discuss the point at this current stage, as I had just told them I was counting on them.

"Here is how these two days are going to look like," I continued my opening statement, and presented the schedule:

Day one:

- Sixty-second introductions, according to the photo page you have prepared
- Presentation of the groups, according to your preparations
- Lunch
- Definition of the common organizational objectives — thirty minutes
- Definition of organizational structures — two hours (in groups)
- Presentation of organizational structures — two hours
- Dinner + fun event

Day two:

- Setting success criteria — one hour
- Rating structures by criteria (in groups)
- Presentation of ratings + discussion
- Selecting a structure

The room fell silent, and the people present tried to follow the events that were supposed to fill the following couple days. They seemed quite confused and waited to see how things would evolve.

We started getting to know one another with personal photographs. It was nice and breezy and allowed everyone to talk and tell stories about themselves, making everyone more comfortable.

We continued to presentations of the different groups. We only answered clarification questions and did not allow any criticism. Everyone was interested, and we learned a lot from one another.

Upon our return from lunch, I presented a page and said: "These are the objectives of our new organization, as I see them:

- An excellent engineering group, that makes any business organization desire that we make its products;
- Effective engineering work, while efficiently using people and tools;
- An organization that everyone wants to be part of.

"What do you think? What should be added? What should be cut down?"

My questions raised a short conversation that mostly included an attempt to understand the significance of each of the parts, and details whenever necessary. By the end of this conversation, we agreed on the group's success principles.

"Now we divide into four groups." I had divided the people into groups in advance, meticulously. It was important to make sure that every group represented all the organizations that existed today, in order to guarantee an effective conversation that included all the projects. This partition was crucial to ensure each group had the knowledge required in their definition of the new structure.

"Does everyone agree on the organization's objectives? Should anything be amended?" All parties present agreed and waited quietly to see how this would unfold.

"Now each of the groups I defined will work for two hours to suggest the correct structure that facilitates achieving the organizational objectives. When you return here, you will have to explain, on a single page, what the structure is that you defined, why you chose it and how it meets the organizational objectives. And a small reminder before you go: Remember to focus on what is right for the organization, detaching your personal role."

Everyone understood and went to their groups.

Sivan, the HR representative, came to me and whispered: "Do you really believe they will detach, and not think about their own job?"

"I don't know if they will succeed, and certainly not everyone will succeed to the same extent, but this is my expectation from senior managers, and it is important to emphasize," I replied. Naturally, I had my own doubts.

After about two hours, the groups returned to the room, with one major complaint: "We wish we had more time to talk."

"I think you had plenty of time, and we will continue the conversation together," I replied, to allow the beginning of the presentations.

The first group presented. After a short while, an argument started, and each of the parties present tried to explain why the option was not good. I stopped the arguments immediately and aimed for clarification questions—if the model is clear, you do not comment on it, even if you disagree with it. This was not simple. Each group was sure of their concept and wanted to convince others. I dealt with deflecting criticism and allowing questions only from people who wanted clarifications.

After a few hours of conversation, we had five possible models for the organizational structure. Even though there were four groups, one of the groups could not agree and presented two models and the disagreement they'd had. It was fine with me. My objective was that they think, that they see that there are a few possible solutions and that they know how to clearly explain their disagreement.

Without a doubt, this was a long and exhausting day for everyone. Everyone was tense, had worked in groups where no one knew the others and had made excellent recommendations. All this—before we had begun evaluating what was better and why, and before we had even debated and made a decision. This was a good time for dinner and for some fun.

We met for dinner, to which I had arranged a short performance by a "senses" artist. The show was stunning and left everyone speechless, even ones who had declared that they did not believe in such nonsense. The atmosphere was open and fun, and this ended the first busy day.

The following morning, everyone was still busy trying to figure out the magic tricks they had experienced the night before. The atmosphere was great, fitting for the day ahead of us, which included plenty of explanations, arguments, convincing and decision-making.

"Good morning; I hope everyone enjoyed themselves yesterday," I opened the day. "Here is a summary of the five models we saw yesterday." I briefly went over the major principles of each of the proposals. "These are the criteria that we agreed lead to the success of the entire organization. Does anyone have any additions? Comments? Changes?"

After a short conversation and some clarifications, we agreed on the criteria.

"This is the rating table," I continued, presenting a table whose lines were dedicated to the criteria and whose columns were dedicated to the five suggested models. "Each cube in the table should be ranked:

"If the model helps in meeting the criterion — mark green;

"If the model makes it difficult to meet the criterion — mark red;

"If the model does not influence meeting the criterion — mark yellow."

Everybody was ready and moved as if to join their former groups. "No, wait; these are the groups you are going to work with now," I presented a new division and verified that each group had a representative of each model. My objective was to have someone explain and justify each model, to make the rating as accurate as possible. It was important that I could guarantee the understanding of the models as they were ranked.

Everyone went to their new groups and started ranking. Sivan came to me and asked, with great fear: "What happens if they are unable to unite under a single model? What happens if there will only be disagreement? There are so many options and opinions—how do you even know it will work?"

Obviously, I had no clear answers to every fear, and I did not know whether it would work. "Sivan, I don't know whether things will form a single model. In any case, we will have a discussion and hear the different opinions; and, ultimately, I will make a decision about the organizational structure."

After about two hours, I gathered all the groups in the main room to review the ratings they had made. The room was filled with tension; everyone wanted their model to be selected; and there were some managers who looked genuinely upset. I was slightly afraid of the quarrels and egoistic fights, but at this point I had no choice; I continued according to my plan.

"Let's review the criteria we defined for the success of the organization," I started, to get everybody back to a joint-consent point. "And now, let's move on to your ratings. Who wants to go first?"

Bob volunteered to start with his group; he presented the table and started his explanations. After a short time, arguments filled the room; and many people tried to explain why his concept was wrong.

"Hold on; there is no right or wrong," I stopped the debate. "This is a rating done by a specific group, and another group can rate differently, and that's fine. Let's focus on understanding the reason for this rating—what they found that was very good and what they found that was disturbing." In this way, all the groups presented their ratings; and the whole time, I tried to steer the conversation to being as objective as possible, to make people realize how other groups think and why. After all the groups had presented their ratings, the picture was quite clear. All the ratings created a single central model, and only one function remained having two options.

This might be surprising, but when objectives are defined and there is an understanding about the abilities of each group, the correct structure is formed—and there are not many options that contradict one another.

After a short break in which I summarized the ratings in a single table, we reconvened, to summarize the past two days.

"Thank you very much for your good work and cooperation. Here is the chosen model: The structure of 'targeting groups by specialization' was agreed upon by all. The central group that supports tools and will help in sharing and efficiency was agreed upon by most. A dispute remains about the location of shared units; and I will decide on that—based on the group evaluations." Up to this point, no factor regarding specific people or abilities had been discussed.

"From this point, I will continue conversations with relevant managers for specific roles according to the model you have defined and on which we have agreed together. Good luck, everyone."

This ended two concentrated and tiring days that had brought about excellent results.

The first and most important one was that we had found a

new structure for the organization, which was more fitting to its needs; and it had been done effectively, supported by the senior, key people of the organization.

The second outcome was that all the employees who participated in the convention would later serve as ambassadors of good will for the entire organization and would be able to explain why this structure had been chosen. This is a great help when you strive to make a change, especially when seeking a quick change.

The third outcome was that the most-senior managers saw and experienced the reasoning and difficulties firsthand. They understood the different sides of the debate and were parties in the process. This would allow them to support the decision even if they were not greatly "fond" of it. A person who understands the challenges is more open to accept any decision and agree to compromises.

Another result is the (relatively quick, due to the intensity of these two days) formation of a collection of senior managers who would have to cooperate sometime in the future.

The organization that operated within this structure was most successful.

A few of the principles of this method and the reasons for its success:

1. Sharing with people the solution to the complex problems that affect them brings about better results. They understand the difficulty and feel like partners to the solution. In cases where most managers are young and inexperienced, this is a chance to provide them with trust, increase their self-esteem and show them they are trusted with a complex process.

   • Share the problem with more senior employees, even if they are not the ones who will take part in the senior management team in the next step.

2. An objective process, detached from specific people, generates an optimal result. In the process of organizational creation, it is important to first define the correct structure, the optimal organization, which will function and create good and efficient results. The people, abilities and connections will be added to the optimal structure. It is possible to make adjustments when necessary, but it is important to stay as close as possible to the original optimal structure.

   • Each group for model building should include representation of all projects.

- Make a different division for ratings that represents all the models.

- During focused conversations about the structure, emphasize the reasons for the recommendation and avoid "right" or "wrong" judgment calls.

- Define and agree upon the criteria for the success of the group. It is important to create consent whenever possible.

When the objectives are clear and shared, it is possible to reach an understanding and better solutions.

3. Lead the process openly, with attention and focus, while maintaining the "correct conversation." The comments and responses during such conversations are vital to success.

- I had no known organizational structure in mind. Everything was open to true conversation. Not even I knew the correct answer, and this allowed me to be open.

- Practice complete concentration in every conversation, in every word. Constantly try to understand one another and avoid judgement.

- Think about and plan all the details in advance, including the evening event—something fun to bring people together and make them feel comfortable. The event was a crucial part of our success. On the first day we started with introductions, with building agreements and common ground.

We continued the day with a structure proposal, which had a judgmental element but was still conducted in small groups. In the evening, it was amusing and unifying—a good and pleasant atmosphere before the arguing, convincing and disagreeing about the assessment of the models.

This is a complex process whose aim is to effectively and objectively define the correct structure, done in a collaborative manner. Everything was done with the heart and soul, and with a significant focus on objectives and results. The sharing and caring, the connections between people and the difficulties created a great experience of commitment and partnership for the people. When things are done with your heart and soul, you engage the people and get the others' hearts and souls in return, and without a doubt, this is a very good result.

I used this model a few times later, in similar situations, and it always succeeded in connecting people, while defining the correct organizational structure for that group. When I taught other managers how to use this model, I explained the emphasis on the different stages and the correct development of the details; and they always got excellent results in group structuring and in extracting true contributions from their employees.

Insights and Applications

- The effective process to define an organizational structure in four stages:
  1. Present areas of responsibility for each group — learning;
  2. Define the criteria for organizational success — joint consent;
  3. Divide into groups to build the models — making suggestions for an organizational structure;
  4. Rate the models according to how they match with the success criteria and choose a structure.
- Emphasize all the details and create a good, fun vibe before the fourth stage in order to enable an efficient and honorable discussion.
- The host should always be alert, while avoiding judgment and maintaining sincerity, allowing for a genuine, deep conversation.

3

PERSONAL ATTITUDE

One of the most important and effective things in creating a sense of partnership and loyalty among group members is the way the leader cares for the people and the group. Many leaders tell me confidently: I care a lot about my group; I worry about them. But honestly, often, they do not know how to show it or how to give people the feeling their well-being is truly important. I believe that caring and concern are very important, but it is as important to show it in small things that make the employees feel you care.

I will demonstrate my point with a few simple stories.

Close to the Heart

Yossi is an experienced engineer who joined our group a few months ago. The day of our first encounter was, unfortunately, relatively late. I did not know him at all; all I knew was that he was an excellent engineer, quiet and shy.

"Hello, welcome to the group," I started the conversation.

"Hello," Yossi answered.

"How are you? What is new?" I kept going, trying to make him talk and be less official.

"I'm fine. My first granddaughter was born," he answered, and I could see the excitement and joy in his eyes.

"Congratulations! How is she? And what is her name?" I followed his lead.

"Everything's fine. Her name is Yael," he answered briefly and to the point, as he had answered all my questions.

"Great! Do you have any pictures? Any proud grandfather carries his granddaughter's pictures on his smartphone; let me see," I carried on.

Yossi enthusiastically took his smartphone out of his pocket, with a large smile on his face. He started showing me pictures of the baby, and I felt how he became more at ease. He took pride in his granddaughter and started to tell me how cute she is, and how she would turn to face him when she hears his voice.

"Congratulations!" I smiled. "Enjoy her. And how is it going in our group?" I shifted the course of our conversation back to work.

By now, he was more open. He told me what was going well at work; we talked about the difficulties and about the help he needs. I did not see quiet and shy Yossi anymore; instead, I saw a kind, open and businesslike individual. I told him about the next steps and concluded: "Do not forget, next time we meet, to bring me updated pictures of Yael, your granddaughter."

"Sure," he smiled. "I will not forget. Goodbye and thanks."

In this story we saw how a personal approach and true interest in a person and in the things important to him, it is possible to generate openness that brings about an open work conversation. A personal approach and openness are highly important for the success of your work, for performing your tasks and for overcoming difficulties.

Professional and Introverted

Nir had been managing the group for quite some time; everyone knew he was highly professional, tough and introverted. Even the people who had worked with him for quite some time knew almost nothing about his family, his children, his hobbies—in fact, they knew nothing of his private life. Only when I became his boss did I really understand what people were talking about; all the conversations I held with him were no-nonsense – even too much so – serious, with no smiles, and he never diverted from the topic of conversation.

Usually, when I talk to employees, I tend to make jokes and talk about things not purely related to work; but with Nir, it was extremely difficult. Any attempt I made to divert the conversation failed. Nir always answered briefly and to the point, and only with regard to work. One morning, he called me and said, "I won't be at work today. Last night we had a daughter." I was shocked. I never knew they were expecting. I quickly came to my senses and answered, "Congratulations! How wonderful! Is everyone OK? Don't come; stay with your wife and children; help and do whatever is needed. We will be just fine here."

He answered briefly: "Thanks, I will be there tomorrow."

When he arrived the next day, I immediately went to congratulate him and asked if there were any pictures and whether I could see his precious daughter. "No pictures, sorry," he answered as usual. "I did not have the chance."

"No problem; everything is fine. When you have pictures, come and show us."

Since that day, every time we met, I asked him about the new baby and how his older children were getting along with her, and took an interest in his wife. Slowly and gradually, Nir started to tell me more, until one day, he entered the room and said, "Look." He immediately took out his phone with the baby's photo collection and showed it to me. "She is so cute!" I enthused, "so big—and look at her smile." I was very happy he had shared with me, and it was important for me to show it. It was important I show that I was happy for him and pleased that he was comfortable sharing with me. Of course, then we went on to talk about work; and only now was he more at ease. At the end of the meeting, I suggested, "From now on, in every meeting, show me an updated picture of your daughter." Smiling shyly, but pleased, he said, "With great joy! Goodbye," and left the room.

This is another example that emphasizes the importance of giving attention to someone else, to his situation, to the things that occupy him and to being with him in that place. It is important to talk about it—about the things that are bothering him or that he is occupied with. Then, the person becomes more attentive and more open in work-related conversations, and he also feels his boss genuinely cares about him.

To Invest and to Balance

Towards the end of any project, everyone works hard, invests many hours and makes every effort to complete things on time. One of the groups that was always stressed at the end of a project was the physical design group, whose job it was to make the transition from design to transistors, drawing and connecting all the circuits—the final stage before sending the design to production.

We were approaching the end of such a project; stress levels were very high, as usual, and at the last minute, just a few weeks before the end, there was a substantial change in the electrical plans—one that required the revision of a large and complex unit. The team manager, Rami, was highly motivated and wanted to do everything necessary for the success of the project. His team was also highly dedicated and motivated. After a few rushed meetings and detailed planning, Rami and the group took it upon themselves to realize this entire big change without extending the project's due date. As happy as I was to hear about this, I wanted to make sure it was real and practical, and did not just amounted to enthusiasm and good will. Per my request, they detailed their plan to me: working shifts around the clock, providing a common room for everyone to sit in and to conduct the corrections efficiently and quickly, and dividing the work into small parallel sub-units. The plan seemed stressful but efficient, and I appreciated their efforts greatly. I thanked them for taking on this great task; I asked to arrange the common room and the shifts, and wished them luck.

After about three days of strained work, I went with Rami to visit the common room where everyone was working. The room was full; everyone was sitting at their computers, working vigorously. I thanked everyone for the good work and for their efforts, progress and investment. As I was talking, I saw Shlomo, who was so tired his eyes were almost shut. I stopped talking and turned to Rami, the manager: "Please call a taxi and send Shlomo home to rest right now."

"No, it's fine; don't worry," Shlomo answered. "I apologize."

"There is nothing to apologize for," I said. "I appreciate your efforts; but now, you, go home, get some rest and spend time with your family, and don't be back until the day after tomorrow." I turned to Rami and said: "Don't let him drive right now; call a taxi and get him out of here."

To conclude, I turned to everyone: "Well done for your investment and caring – it is very important and extremely valued – but it is just as important to take care of yourselves and your families. Everyone has to know their own limits and to take time to rest, be with your families and recharge. Good luck with your project— and, Rami, please tend to your employees' break times."

It is always important to create balance between strained work and the need to achieve your objective correctly, and worrying about individual interests and setting reasonable targets. It was obvious that if the employees vigorously worked overtime, the work would progress faster; but when a person reaches such a level of tiredness, it is important to take care of him and to let him rest. The fact I had said it in front of everyone allowed people to see and feel how much every employee was important to me—just as important as the task at hand.

New Hobbies

"Nathan, how are you? You seem troubled," I said, as Nathan entered the room Monday morning.

"Everything's fine," he said. "Just a bunch of things you naturally don't care about. My soccer team really screwed up yesterday, and the game sucked," he continued talking, looking disappointed.

"I do want to know. What happened? Why did they screw up?" I continued, "but you should really spell it out for me, as I understand nothing about soccer."

"Yesterday was a really important game," Nathan said, "and the team sucked. This is the second time they forfeited with a large gap, and according to the calculations, they are at risk of being demoted from the league."

I tried to understand the scoring system, and how they summarized the games; and Nathan explained everything patiently and to the detail. "So, there is still a chance, if I understand things correctly; not all is lost," I tried to cheer him up. "Let's hope their next game is better."

"Yes, let's hope," Nathan answered. "It will be fine—it's really nice you take an interest in soccer," he laughed.

"As you saw," I said, "I don't understand much, but it's always good to hear an explanation and learn something new." We went on to talk about work, and Nathan seemed much more available.

International Personal Relationships

Personal relationships within a group that extends between countries and continents are complex and important for the success of complex projects that are done by a few groups. When we consider the attitude between the manager and the team, the way to initiate a sense of proximity and caring is rather simple—fly abroad to visit the team and hold personal face-to-face meetings with its members. Creating relationships and familiarity between team members and having personal relationships with them is far more complex when the group is divided between continents, as it is impossible to fly the entire group.

When I was managing the YAM project, it was the first time I received an American group which became part of my organization and had to work closely with the Israeli group. Obviously, at the start of the project, I defined areas of responsibility for each team, and then we defined the methodology and shared work methods. Right from the start, it was obvious that there were differences in the work methods and methodology—and this generated many tensions. I tried to think about how we could initiate familiarity, trust and personal relationships between people, simply and quickly before the rifts and disagreements grew. I consulted my HR partner, Nurit. Nurit suggested we create an international acquaintance game in mixed groups. I was enthusiastic about the concept, and we created the game:

At first, we collected special hobbies from team members—or a funny or odd event that had happened to them. These are short items, which can be described in a single line. We used this to generate a long list of questions; and the team members were divided into groups of four (in total, the organization had about 300 people—so, many groups were formed), with the objective to guess whose line each was. Naturally, the first group who correctly guessed all the names would win the game. As a hint, we told them to think about the way they create groups: You might feel more comfortable with people whom you know and who work at the same office, but then the chances of finding out more about other people are lower. On the one hand, it is more difficult to create mixed groups when you are not familiar with anyone—but it provides a greater chance of success. In a short while, groups were formed, and a great number of them were mixed with people who had had no former acquaintance. For three weeks, the game kept going; the groups held meetings to keep up to date, to divide the tasks between them, to check scores—and after a few tries, there was a winning team that got the reward.

The game was simple and easy to set up, and it achieved many important objectives for the team. First of all, according to the original objective, people got to know one another personally—hobbies, experiences and other things not related to work. Within the group, there were acquaintanceships and friendships, because people were talking among themselves a lot – sometimes in their off-hours – sharing various experiences and enjoying the common discovery. When you have a common objective which is also fun, a personal bond is created easily and naturally. Such familiarity is a critical component of success when you get to needing to solve difficult problems and to defuse stressful situations, and it helps everyone to cooperate a little more.

Another just-as-important advantage is that they experienced how to make international sharing convenient and simple. They initiated the sessions, experienced the difficulties of coordinating meetings, and handled time differences and other constraints. They understood how important it is to be clear about the way you divide the work in order to progress as quickly as possible.

In addition, the group members discovered the advantage of working in mixed groups, where there are different knowledge bases and connections. Indeed, mixed groups got to the correct answers faster.

It is known that people tend to be caring and loyal when they feel they are looked after and that another person cares about them. In these examples, it was evident that by using small talk with an employee, taking an interest in their families, their hobbies, their own well-being (for instance, that they rest first and drive later), employees could feel that we really cared about them and about the things important to them in that moment. Consideration and taking care of others does not decrease the demand for high performance, for meeting deadlines and for maintaining high quality, but they come hand in hand with such demands. Using simple small talk, I was always able to mobilize people for the task—even when it was difficult and exceedingly complicated. I was able to make them truly care about the project, the group and the outcome. These two strategies – high expectations together with plenty of caring generate an excellent atmosphere that allows for high-quality results.

Creating good personal relations between the staff themselves further improves the sense of belonging and allows for cooperation in complex tasks and for the solution of difficult problems.

Insights and Applications

- It is important to show that you genuinely care about the other person.

- It is important to take interest in the person, his family, his hobbies and everything that matters to him.

- Maintaining demands for high performance while genuinely caring for every employee generates real trust that gets better engagement and results.

- By using simple processes (such as a game), you can generate personal relationships between group members, even when the members are spread between various continents. It is important to conduct this process early on, when creating the group, before there are rifts or misconceptions between group members.

4

BENEFICIAL BEHAVIOR AND SOLUTIONS IN STRESSFUL SITUATIONS

In the book of greetings I received when I retired from Intel, people wrote about me: "brilliant engineer, strong leader and, primarily, a human being." I believe that all these things should coexist. Sometimes, it seems that one thing supplants the other; but the ability to be a human being and a manager with high expectations and effective solutions under stress is highly important in leading a group to succeed in complex tasks. At work, you come across many stressful situations, including malfunctions, surprises and things that do not go according to plan. The way you handle these situations significantly influences your work organization, your outcomes and the group's engagement and level of motivation.

Any finalization of a project is a stressful time. This stage is called Tape Out (TO). During this time, everyone works hard, conducts all the tests and verifies that no mistakes were sent to manufacturing. Everybody invests plenty of work hours. The GRP project

I managed was exceedingly complex (at that time), as it had to be integrated with graphics for the first time and was greatly dependent upon groups in Israel and the United States. It was the first time such a complex project was done in Israel, and the first time for me, as manager of such a project. Along the way, we came across plenty of hardships: We failed to reach milestones on time; sometimes, we reached them a few months too late; and we had plenty of status meetings with our boss, Shaul. Shaul was highly professional, setting very high standards. The meetings with him were difficult and stressful. Before these meetings, we would work for a long time to prepare the materials, and yet there were many problems. Most meetings ended with comments such as: "You should finish all simulations on time, and you have plenty;" "I don't understand why you did not find enough bugs;" "How are you going to achieve milestones with all the open issues?"

After each session, I was desperate and disappointed. Again, he only mentioned missing things; again, he only discussed problems. Wasn't it possible that we had done something good? Why did he not mention that? People had worked so hard, so why did he not mention it? Why did he only complain? But for the group, I always tried to summarize it in a positive, balanced way: "We have plenty of work to do, and we must finish the simulation by the end of the week. I can see that during the past few weeks, there was good progress, and I am sure that if we keep this up, we will be able to finish the required simulations. Tell me what you need in order to progress faster." I knew I should never transmit only the stress to the group, only the notes about missing pieces and the insults I'd experienced. It was very important for me to maintain high motivation, to cheer them on, to help them have the will and the energy to keep on investing.

This complex period carried on throughout the entire last year of our work on the project; and now, finally, we were approaching the TO. Everyone was working on final tests and fixing any bug they found, as quickly as possible. On Thursday, we found ourselves going through the entire database structure; and I was waiting for the results on Friday morning, so I could approve the project for manufacturing.

"Shlomit, we must hold a meeting ASAP—there is a big problem," Tamir, the silicon test manager told me. We immediately sent for the relevant people, and I came to hear what the problem was. "We found that the tests for the first silicon are not ready and that we cannot test to see what is working once the component is manufactured," Tamir started the meeting. I was shocked by the news; how come we figured this out only now? We had never conducted a TO without being prepared with such tests. Immediately, a million options came to my mind, and they all seemed worse than the last: We would prepare the tests and only then TO; this is what we always did—impossible, this would delay us greatly; we were already behind schedule; everyone was waiting for the TO and knew it should be out today. Shaul, the boss, would kill me for such a delay. We would TO without the test—impossible; this was never done; no one would allow us. Was there any way to prepare the tests quickly and only be late by one day? Who knew if it were possible?

These thoughts and many more went through my mind, but I was in a meeting with eight people who had just now told me about the problem and were waiting to hear from me about what should be done and about what the next steps would be. I started referring questions to others who were sitting in the room: "How long would it take to prepare the tests?"

"Unclear. It will be complicated due to the new integration," the experts answered.

"Is there a similar project we can borrow the tests from, and change them slightly?" I asked further.

"No, there is no such project. The most similar project uses other tools, and we cannot take prepared tests from there; everything demands redefining."

The problem was brand new, and yet people expected me to provide a solution or a direction regarding what should be done. One of the ways that greatly helps in focusing a problem is to ask questions. I always ask questions to understand the facts and the situation at hand. I ask questions to make people think about other things, other directions, other options—to see the bigger picture. I ask questions to make the group a part of the solution, to motivate them, to allow them to be partners in success. The questions would help in many ways, in this case, to achieve the goal. I had understood the problem and the fact that there would be no shortcuts on the way to solving it.

To benefit the most from questions, it is important they be "good questions." Good questions, according to my definition, should be FBI questions:

Focused: The questions should be focused on the issue and the problem.

Because: The reason for the questions should be clear, and you should know what you want to make of the answer. An unfocused question does not achieve anything, and sometimes seems irrational or annoying to the individual answering it.

Intent: There should be a true intent to use the answer to the question in your conversation, or in solving the problem. A truly authentic question is one asked not merely for the sake of asking, not only to know more details.

When these three principles exist in questions, they enable the achievement of all the objectives: 1) focusing on the problem; 2) conducting a greater and clearer examination of the entire situation and its meaning; 3) building motivation and cooperation toward the success of the task or toward the solution of the problem.

"OK, so we are going to work simultaneously," I said. "We have a few weeks until this returns from manufacturing, and during that time, we have to verify that all the tests have been prepared. We will send it to TO tomorrow, as planned, after I clear it with the boss." I knew it was going to be one of the toughest things I had to do, but I carried on: "Today, right now, Tamir will set up a group of the best test experts, who will be dedicated to this task, with a clear objective to have the tests ready on the first day out of manufacturing. Are there any questions? Anyone unclear about the next stages?" I summarized all the stages briefly to allow them to carry on with their work.

Within the silence in the room, it was possible to hear a sigh of relief from some people. As they left the room, they whispered: "Yes, simultaneous work is very sensible." Others said: "This ended well; no one killed us. Now we must go get all the tests ready; it will not be simple, but we promised." I felt that everyone understood the magnitude of their mistake, and nevertheless, everyone had been recruited to do everything they could to make it work this time around.

The mistake was obvious, and perhaps it was even a huge mistake. I decided not to deal with the question about whose fault it was and why it happened. I took responsibility so that we could progress and focus on the solution. Learning would be highly important for the next project, but in such a stressful situation, there was not enough time; and it would be wrong to add the pressure of searching for guilty parties. To achieve maximum cooperation, we all focused on what we would do next – what should be done to achieve the objective – and the entire responsibility was upon management, but not within the group.

At the end of the project, as we did a postmortem, this was

obviously one of the issues that arose; and we learned how to better prepare and have all the tests ready once the component had left the manufacturing stage. The fact that this conversation was had once there was already a solution to the problem – and that everyone knew no one was looking for someone to blame but, instead, that there was a genuine motivation to learn – highly contributed to having an effective conversation and taught us for the future.

On my way to my boss, Shaul, to get his approval, I knew it would be a brutal conversation. He was not fond of surprises and especially not surprises of this kind; everything had to be according to plan, according to established and familiar stages. I knew that the next day, Shaul was scheduled to go abroad; so, it was clear to me that I had to find him that day and get his approval. "Shaul, when do you have time today? I must speak with you before you go."

Shaul, who was standing in the hallway next to my cubicle, answered, "Yes, what's the problem? Let's talk now."

"I realized today that there has been a mistake and that they never prepared the silicon tests."

"What? And only now you know about it?! How are you planning TO for this weekend if there are no prepared tests yet?" Anger was showing on his face, and he was right to be upset.

I started stuttering, "Yes, this is a real bummer, but I don't know if it is worth holding back the TO again for this."

"What good is the silicon without the tests? How will you know it's working? This is just what I needed—more delays for the TO," Shaul said.

"I thought we could work in parallel," I offered. "We will send for TO tomorrow as planned, and until we get the silicon, we have a few more weeks in which we can prepare the tests."

"How do you know it will be on time? And what if it doesn't work?" Shaul asked.

"I've put together a team of experts, and this is the only thing they will work on from now until the silicon gets here," I carried on explaining my plan.

"I don't know what to tell you; this is a real mess. Tomorrow, I have to go, so do whatever you want." He ended the conversation sounding desperate and angry.

I felt alone and confused. On the one hand, I believed that my plan was good. On the other hand, Shaul was not supporting me and did not have my back. But, then again, he did say, "Do whatever you want," so why not carry on in the direction I believed in?

Pondering and worried about what to decide, I went home, constantly deliberating about what I should do. I had no one to consult with; no one I knew was in such a situation and could tell me what to do. Shaul, my boss, was very angry, and he was going to be on the plane for the next twenty-four hours, so I couldn't talk to him either.

On Friday morning, as planned, the news that the TO runs ended successfully came in, and I had to authorize the manufacturing. I was scared; this was a huge expense for the company; everyone was waiting for it, keeping tabs on the project—and what if the tests were not ready on time? But I believed that, in our situation, the right thing to do was to carry on with my plan and perform the TO.

After all my deliberations, it was highly important that I decide. I had come to the best decision possible based on the data I had had, understanding the risks involved and taking them into account. I had asked what would happen if we were not ready with the tests—would it still be worthwhile to approve? Yes, I'd answered—because the time span is long, and if worse came to worst, we would begin with partial tests—but that would be better than postponing the entire thing.

In complex situations, some people wait for more data and avoid making any decisions; but in most cases, this just makes the situation worse. In fact, avoiding a decision means continuing what we have done so far, even though we never determined why it is right. I think this is the worst solution—and it is even worse than making a decision that is wrong but is one we had thought about, understanding its importance and the risks it entails. It is important to take all options and risks into account, and then decide, while understanding the possible outcomes. This is how I reached this decision; and eventually it brought about positive outcomes. It is lucky I decided to TO.

Many weeks later, the component arrived and some of the tests were ready. Not all the tests, as we had planned, but more than fifty percent of them. With the available tests, we started the first silicon testing and discovered a critical error that required an immediate fix. We sent the fix to manufacturing right away—and, I thought, how lucky it was that we worked in parallel, as it allowed us to find the problem sooner and save plenty of precious time.

Handling a complex situation, you should use all your knowledge and engineering know-how to understand the situation, the risk, the possible solutions. You should be strong and withstand the stress, deal with assertions and anger from your superiors, and yet be understanding and supportive of the people who found the problem and have to work on fixing it.

Integrating strength, emotion and understanding allows for better, more creative solutions and, without a doubt, generates limitless trust and loyalty in people, which brings about successful outcomes.

Insights and Applications

- In strained, stressful work, it is important to provide positive energy to your team and to motivate them to continue; it is highly important to demonstrate your appreciation for the work done and to mention what progressed, while not letting go of your high expectations or what is missing.

- "FBI" (Focus, Because, Intent) questions focus on the real problem at hand, clarify complexities, open the possibility to think about different directions and new solutions, and make people become a part of the solution.

- After a specific problem has been solved, identify the reasons it happened in the first place and draw conclusions to prevent it from happening again.

- It is important to reach clear decisions, knowing the advantages and the risks of any option. Avoiding a decision is the worst; it is like deciding without considering the advantages and risks.

5

A DIFFICULT MESSAGE

Udi, the model-integration manager, worked very hard throughout the entire project. His work required cooperation with many people, coordination of tasks, and the ability to solve problems and to work around them when a solution was unavailable. Since models were central to the project, there was always great pressure to get the job done, and Udi had to update everyone about this progress. The job was vital, and Udi enjoyed his central position in the project, investing many hours—but not always getting the required outcomes.

On the one hand, Udi received cooperation from friends: "Do this now, and I will help you later." On the other hand, he was highly aggressive when he did not receive the help he requested. Throughout the entire project, and as the task grew and became more complicated, things were delayed, and it was essential to think differently, to improve the work method, to build the solution in an organized manner, to create the right structure for the employees and to generate positive cooperation. This type of change less suited Udi's character, and he was unable to bring it about.

Udi was caring and devoted, but he pushed harder and harder—arguing, becoming increasingly aggressive with people and harsher in requesting help. All these things did not really improve the situation and spurred debate within the team, rather than strengthening the team's cooperation. About halfway through the project, at a critical point, I decided that I would manage the model integration with Udi. I held a conversation with him to illuminate the problematic aspects in his behavior and the change I wished to make.

"Udi, we need to improve the integration of the models and make it faster, because it delays the entire project," I said.

"Right; I understand," he answered, "but Rachel is not supplying the ready-made tools, and Dan does not give updates on time; it is not up to me."

"I understand there is great dependency and that the task at hand is brutal; but it is your job as task manager to solve the problems and make others cooperate with you. Since the tension between people is too high, I will intervene, run daily meetings and move this task forward. You are still responsible for model integration, and I will help you work with the various groups to get their cooperation and to set priorities for various tasks."

"Fine—but I am not really sure this will work," said Udi.

"I don't know in advance how much it will help, but something needs to be done differently, and we have to try everything in order to solve the issues. It is impossible to carry on like we're doing. We will try and, over time, we shall see what needs to be improved," I continued.

Udi left the room looking disappointed, as he had been deprived of his crucial role in the project. I understood his disappointment, but it was clear that something needed to be changed and done differently, and looking at the bigger picture, I had to see the entire project and the interests of all people and not just a single individual.

The next morning, I had already started scheduling coordination and synchronization meetings. I always took care to emphasize Udi's part and give him clear tasks. At first, Udi's work was lacking passion; but very quickly, when he saw things were progressing, he dived into things and started moving through the tasks quickly.

At the end of the project, Udi's team had to expand in terms of its tasks, working on a few projects in parallel and working on more complex, longer tasks. I learned throughout the project that, on the one hand, Udi was not the right person to lead a large organization with serious long-term challenges; but on the other hand, he did put in plenty of energy and long hours, and was caring and highly motivated. He was not pleased that I had gotten involved with the model integration, but he carried on making a great effort and guaranteeing the mission's success.

Haim was a younger manager in the group, and he had proved himself with all the tasks he had received and always worked great with the group, both in terms of people and in terms of tasks. I thought Haim would be suitable to replace Udi in managing the team, and that I should define a more technical role for Udi, so that he would succeed in it better.

I was stuck between a rock and a hard place. What was the right thing to do?

For the benefit of the team, it was obvious that there was a need for a different type of manager, someone who was more structured, more organized—that could handle complexities in a better way. For Udi's benefit, I should let him keep on growing, providing him with opportunities and recognition in all the efforts he had made. I spent long days deliberating on what the right thing to do was, and each day, I was able to convince myself of the opposite. In such cases, there is no one really to consult with, as the careers of the people working for the organization are at stake. Despite all my deliberations, I had to decide. It is known that not deciding is a decision on its own, since the current situation remains, and it is not always the proper solution.

The next project was about to start, and I had to create a team. I had to reach a decision.

I started working to create the change. First, I checked around to see if Haim really wanted the job. I did not tell him anything for sure; I only asked if he would be interested in a management position should he be given the option. I explained to Haim what the role would entail, to ensure that he did not reach his decision lightly, and after a day, he returned to me and said, "I don't think it is relevant, because Udi is there; but if there were such a role, I would be really interested in it."

I calmed down a bit, because I had come up with a good solution; but the difficult conversation was yet to come. How would I deliver Udi a message about replacing him, in a dignified manner, without hurting his feelings?

I invited Udi for a talk.

"Now that the project is over, we need to continue to build the group for the following tasks and challenges," I told him. "We have plenty of new and complex projects, and in order to succeed, we need to have a more organized, structured work system, with long-term planning."

Udi looked at me and listened, but it was apparent that he did not have a clue about what I wanted from this conversation.

I continued, "You are excellent at storming into tasks, at putting out fires, at making everyone tick at the last moment; but organized work with long-term plans is more difficult for you."

"Right," Udi answered. "It is always important I solve the immediate problems as quickly as possible; but in the long term, there is not too much planning, since everything changes."

"When there are many tasks and people working simultaneously on a few projects, it's important to plan ahead and build the group correctly, so that the plan is clear to any individual in the group and to external parties. To succeed with a group growing at a pace more rapid than expected, I thought about appointing a new manager more suited to coping with this kind of challenge and to give you a job more fitting for your abilities."

The room fell silent. Udi looked at me for a second and did not say a word, but soon he came to his senses and angrily said, "That is not true; I can manage a bigger group, and I am not willing to move to any other job."

"I understand that you dislike the concept," I said, "but as I explained, this is the right thing for you and for the entire group."

"Why are you saying I am a bad manager? After everything I invested in model integrations in the last project, why shouldn't I get a bigger group?"

"It is true – you are highly devoted and caring, and this is important for your success – but for the group expansion and for multiple projects, there are other traits that are not your strengths as much."

"That is untrue. I can manage a large group; let me try, and see for yourself," Udi answered.

At this point, Udi was angry, and I felt that the conversation was neither progressing nor beneficial.

"I suggest we each think about the conversation from various angles and meet again in a few days," I said.

Udi left the room upset, and I stayed, a heavy feeling settling in. It was clear to me that Udi considered this a personal attack, and that was not my intent. I thought it would be good for him to fill a suitable role. It was clear to me that I had to care for the entire organization; I must make the group a success, to have the people know what they should do, to have the people and the organization develop in their work methods. Every leader must take care of the people in the organization and also take care of the organization as a whole. When both goals go together, the direction is clear. But, in many cases, the sides are in conflict, and then the leader must handle the conflict—to create a correct balance, to weigh the gains and losses of every option, and then to decide. In this case, I saw a greater importance in organizational needs, because the status of the organization would have a greater influence on people, and on the company's outcomes and its success. The risk that Udi would be dissatisfied still existed, but I decided it was the right price to pay, and that was the reason I continued with the change I had determined.

We both had a few rough days – each of us had his own deliberations – and then we met again.

"How are you?" I asked. "What were your thoughts?"

"If you don't want me here, I will leave and go home," Udi answered.

"That was not the message I was trying to deliver; I don't think you need to leave. I do believe that you too will be better off in a role more suited to your abilities." The talk went on for another hour or so. Udi tried to explain that he could manage a large group, and I tried to explain his strengths and what was missing for him in fulfilling the role I was evaluating. When we reached a dead end again, I suggested we take some more time to think and meet again in a few days.

After about a week, we met again. "What's up?" I asked.

"Fine; I get it," Udi answered, "but what will my job be?"

I got the feeling that Udi had internalized the situation and wanted to move forward and make sure we had a good solution for him.

"In our group, you can oversee integration. I am also open to helping you find any suitable role in any group in the company."

"No, not in the group. How much time do I have to find a job?" He asked.

"Time is unlimited; we will find the right job for you. We will notify the group of the change within two weeks; and you will stay in the group until you find an interesting role that you want and that fits you."

"Fine. Thanks," he said. "Can you connect me with other groups and managers?" Naturally, I agreed, and promised Udi I would assist him.

The message was delivered. Udi expressed interest in other opportunities, and I referred him to roles more appropriate for him. The process took more than three months until Udi found a group and a job he desired and went on to do it. He was highly successful in his new job and stayed there for many years.

In our group, the new manager began working right after the announcement; he performed his work in a highly organized and defined manner, and enjoyed the cooperation of all the interfaces. The organization succeeded and grew. The process was long and complex at various stages. It was not simple for Udi – who was hurt – and not for me—as the manager leading it. Many managers would say it could have been done much quicker and "why waste time?" They would say I should simply have told Udi to find another role and deal with it. I am happy I took the time and the effort to help Udi understand the message and support him as he found other options.

I strongly believe that behind any role and any mission, there is a human being with desires and emotions. You should always be considerate of the human being in front of you; consider their emotions and work with them, on top of the mission itself. A personal and understanding attitude assists in messages being received, even if they are considerably difficult, and assists in understanding other people's reasons and rationale, even when a decision is not likeable. When an employee is hurt and struggling, it is vital that his manager helps him with emotional particulars, as well – giving him time to process, investing in conversations and explanations –without giving up the principal aim—and by doing the right thing. You should always care about the individual, the human being, in every task and in every decision you make. You should lead with your heart and take the right actions, even when they are difficult.

Insights and Applications

- When delivering a difficult message, respect the person and explain his strengths and his weaknesses.

- At every stage, care for the individual: Provide him with time to process the message and think about solutions. Also, assist him in realizing his solution.

- Even when the message is harsh, you should weigh the good of the individual and the good of the entire organization, and decide upon the solution which has the most critical impact.

6

INITIATING AND DRIVING CHANGE

In management, there are many difficulties, stresses and tensions and a lot of hard work. One of the most challenging tasks, which is yet highly important for success, is leading the organization: the extent to which people agree with the leader, support him, listen to him and follow in his footsteps. Leading an organization towards change is even more difficult. Most people object to changes, and habits are difficult to change. In order to succeed and make a change in the organization, it is important to engage the managers, and then the entire group, and make them believe in the new way. Naturally, the manager decides, and everything goes according to his requests; but as a leader, I don't use words like "do so, because I say so" or "I am the manager, and this is what I said;" I always explain, convince, and want to draw people alongside me, in belief and in partnership—and not just because I said so.

One of the managers who met my mother many years ago said, "I don't know what that lady does; but everyone follows her, through fire and water, to any task." Drawing people into the task at hand, to me, is an important principle, in whatever I do.

"CAN DO"

One of the groups I managed in the States, which had given me a harsh welcome, went through many project cancelations. They had a difficult time progressing to a new project while maintaining their motivation and energy. In most meetings, they all worked hard to explain why it was impossible to do something, why things were not the way they were, why the project could be canceled. Things were so extreme that, one day, when it was announced that the senior business manager was coming for a visit and wanted to see the project status, everyone panicked and explained that he was coming to cancel the entire project. The reason for that visit was the project's high importance; he wanted to make sure that we were ready and that we finished on time, but they understood it completely in the opposite way. I tried to work with them on preparing the materials and explaining the importance of the visit and its purpose, but until the meeting itself, everyone was highly skeptical.

Naturally, I won't say to them, "just work." If you do not believe and if you are not motivated, nothing is possible. However, I always believed that you have to deal with what you have, stop complaining and always do your best—this is the only way to succeed. I explained the project's importance to them repeatedly; we created small milestones they believed they could reach, and together we created the motto "CAN DO."

Whenever I held a team meeting with regular updates on the project's progress, I always added two pages: In the one titled "CAN DO," I mentioned one or two things which were extremely difficult and in which the team had been successful during the past month, to show them that everything was possible. The other was titled "The Challenge," which I used to mention the important, challenging tasks that we were to face in the following month. This habit contributed to the internal belief in the group and led to discussing the interesting things we were doing and the interesting challenges we were facing.

This consistency in mentioning the positive things swept the group into a state of doing and succeeding.

I invested about six months in persuasion and explanations: why things were possible, how things were possible. I searched for simple and practical solutions all the time. With plenty of work and believing with my whole heart, after two years, this group produced a highly successful project. The effort to make people believe it was possible – to keep them motivated, to present small examples and to use them consistently – bore fruit. The group became a highly motivated and capable organization that continued delivering many good projects.

Cutting Down Schedules

When I moved to the big server group, which is a group dealing with designing components for large data centers and communication networks, I had to deal with an entirely different field from the world of laptop computers I had dealt with before. I was starting off, still learning my role. During my second week there, the new manager came to me and said, "You have to look at the ABC project. They are delayed by six months, and we have to solve it right away." As far as I was concerned, this statement was like throwing a bomb on the table. I did not know the people or the project yet. A six-month delay is a long time, and it is hard to solve; but I was new, and it was important for me to succeed in my role.

At first, it seemed like "mission impossible," but I am not familiar with the term "impossible," and just as I was used to getting by on my own, I knew I would do everything the best way I knew how. I immediately went to talk to the group manager and learn the subject. Over the following three days, I participated in endless meetings with both group managers, and all the meetings were to explain why they were working the best way that they could, within the tight schedule and that it was impossible to do anything faster—so, there would be no way to finish the project earlier, as requested.

Without a doubt, this nut was difficult to crack, and what made it more difficult was the strong belief of both managers that it was impossible to do things differently or better. Only, I didn't give up that easily, and after a long debate with myself, I decided to sit with them both and talk about other options, to ask what might help them, assuming anything was possible. For instance—if it were possible to change the rules, what would they change? Or if they could start over, without any constraints, what would they do differently? The objective of these questions was to open their minds to as many options as possible. I believed that this was what would bring about a new solution.

And so, while talking to them, I suddenly asked what would happen if they would perform coding and verification tasks at the same time. Immediately, and without any hesitation, they started to explain why it was not good and was less efficient, and why "this is not how we do things." I listened to what they were saying but continued: "True—this is not as efficient, because we might do some parts over when we check, but it does allow for an opportunity to end the entire task sooner. Would you agree with me?" They listened skeptically and asked a few questions to understand what I meant. I naturally answered everything enthusiastically. Suddenly, the project manager said hesitantly, "It might be possible, but I am not sure we will finish sooner; and it will be difficult for the entire team, because this was not how we have worked." I understood and agreed, but I added, "I know that this is not the way you are used to, but if we divide everything into small tasks, we can explain to people how to get used to it. If this works, it will be a significant accomplishment for the organization and an impressive improvement for the group. If it fails, I am in charge, and in any case, it will not finish later than the current schedule."

They created the plan according to the new principles. We had cut six months off the schedule, all thanks to the parallel execution. The group slowly became accustomed to the new work regime. This was not easy; people worked hard and were obligated to maintain a high quality in their work. Finally, they were able to finish the project by the desired time.

When you believe that you can do things, when you think differently or think you can succeed despite all of the constraints, it is indeed possible. When managers, and then employees, start to believe and really want to succeed in a new method of working, things happen. Today, some of the people think it was their idea and that they never worked differently. This is the best proof for success and the best proof the change was received positively.

For difficult tasks, we must always support, have faith in and generate motivation within the group, to have them give their most and to achieve their best results. To that end, I give some important methods: The first, and perhaps the most important, is listening and understanding. You must hear the group out, listen to the things that are difficult for them and understand what is stalling them. Without getting to the root of the problem or the obstacle, it is difficult to provide a solution which requires a change in group behavior that is convincing and practical for everyone. The second method is to work with the managers and the technical leaders first. There are a few important reasons for this method. First, at initial stages, you have to find the solution together and think about what the right thing to do is. It is important to ensure managers are a part of the solution – that they believe in the direction and know their manager supports them and trusts them – and that if things go wrong, that their manager will assume responsibility. This is the type of security you want to give the leading team when driving changes in the organization. The second reason for this method is that it enables preparation of the way in which the managers will explain to other employees the new way of working and will think together about how to take the entire group to their new destination. Work and preparation with the direct managers assist in harnessing the entire organization for that mission. The third reason is that this is an excellent tool to develop the management, providing them with methods and tools to deal with such cases in the future, so that they know to initiate and push the next change. Eventually, more than performing successful tasks, every leader strives to build and develop the next generation of leaders—to have many more successful leaders.

It is always important to engage the group and the management in the direction set by the leader. Understanding people, relating to problems seriously and with your entire soul, making clear demands and expectations for results—all these enable people to feel like they belong, to believe in their path, to understand the change and to succeed in implementing it.

Insights and Applications

- "CAN DO" — You must always emphasize recent successes and base the next challenge on them.
- Ask open-ended questions to understand difficulties and to open thinking to new possibilities. It is important to be genuinely attentive to the answers and the problems raised and to learn the current situation before offering any changes; this is the way to guarantee a high-quality solution.
- Harness the managers and technical leaders to lead the change and, through them, encourage this change in the entire organization. There are three main reasons for this:
  1. The managers are a part of the solution.
  2. The managers will become "change agents"—the ones motivating change in the organization.
  3. The managers will learn to lead change by themselves and will develop professionally.
- When the new direction succeeds, it is the success of the manager and the team. If there are any problems or malfunctions, the responsibility falls on the leader. It is important to provide the managers in the field with this confidence in order to ease their fear of change.

7

MY LEADERSHIP PRINCIPLES

For many years, I worked and grew within the same organization; people knew me, and I knew them. When I started to lead a group in the Servers organization, I was thinking about a good way for them to get to know me in a short amount of time. Of course, talking about me and my career is always useful to start with; but I was looking for something more, something that is important and unique to me. When preparing for the first meeting with the whole organization, and thinking about my leadership, I understood and then defined three very important leadership principles I use to this day.

1) **People** — This is the most important asset we have in every company. Without people, there is no business and no company. It is known and said by many leaders, "People are the most important asset," but the real question is how it really manifests in the daily work. For me, a demonstration by actions rather than words is important and enables me to show that each employee is important

to me. Most important is the respect I give to people, regardless of their role, grade or position. I do this when they do things right, but also when they do things wrong, even in a disagreement or argument. Investing in people in order to show them the importance of their work, and to help them improve and advance is also an important part of this insight.

In my first management role, we had a student, Ron, that worked on validation coverage. This was a very long task that required attention to details, and it progressed slowly. One day, a customer called and said, "I am stopping all shipments of your product due to its low quality." I was very worried and decided that the first thing was to show them the verification coverage we were doing and the focus that we put on quality. It was clear that we needed to progress faster with the coverage, but just telling Ron to go faster would not be helpful. I decided to show Ron the cruciality and importance of his work. As we had daily conference calls with the clients, I invited Ron to attend one of them. For a student to be in such a conference call with a customer was very unusual, and he was surprised and excited about the opportunity. I told Ron, "You don't need to answer any questions, as I am there to provide answers; you are there just to hear the feedback and impressions from the client." Ron came to the meeting and did not know what to expect. As the meeting started, the client complained about the low quality of the product. I responded clearly that quality was our number one focus, and that we had complete validation coverage whose entire goal is quality. We had milestones for this activity and were willing to update him about the progress on a weekly basis. The client was happy to hear our working plan was focused on quality and asked to be updated twice a week. I naturally agreed, and we ended the meeting. All this time, Ron listened quietly. When we hung up, Ron said, "I see my work is very important, and clients are really looking forward to seeing those results. I'll do my best to work faster as often as I can." "Thank you very much, Ron," I answered. "Just make sure that work does not impact your studies." Ron was pleased to see he was doing meaningful work; I was able to show him the impact he was having on the product (even as a student) and, with his increased effort, there was faster progress in this task.

This is one example showing the importance of the work, how critical the activity is. Enabling Ron to be in the meeting with the client increased his motivation and dedication to putting in all his effort for faster success. At the same time, I made sure to mention that his studies are important, as well. Seeing that his direct manager cares for his personal goals is an additional layer that helps people be dedicated and care about the work as much as the manager cares about their needs. Throughout this book, I gave many examples that show respect and true care for people.

2) **Results** — Every business, and every success, is about business results, whatever the business is. For me, results have a very clear meaning: **Quality On Schedule**. When you focus on the schedule,

since you want to be first in the market, but you don't ensure quality, it is not useful and usually does not work. But on the other hand, when you focus on quality, it might cause delays and a late release of the results; it is far from useful, since competition already controls the market. So, the only REAL Results are Quality on Schedule. To achieve Quality On Schedule, there needs to be clear priorities and a correct balance of the work.

As a leader who managed design and execution activities my entire career, the result concept is very important, clear and simple to explain to all my teams. In a short time, the entire team knows the slogan by heart and the entire organization is operating by it.

3) **Enjoy** — I know I am most successful when I enjoy my work, and this is true for everyone. Naturally, in every job, there are tasks that are more and less likeable – not everything is great –but overall, if we enjoy most of the work (sometimes I say 75 percent, although it is not measurable), then we will succeed, and so will our business and company.

When I had to decide what I would study, I asked my mother's advice, and she had a very short answer: "Go study something you like; I am sure you will succeed." I took her advice, and it worked for me throughout my career: Doing something I like and enjoy enables my greater success.

John, an excellent engineer in my group, was also an expert in his field and asked to talk with me about something not directly related to work. I naturally agreed, and we scheduled a meeting. When John arrived, he opened the discussion. "I would like to be open with you. Please do not use this against me or my work." "Sure, no problem; what's the issue?" I asked.

"In the last few months, I have felt that my designing has not been going well enough. I don't know the reason; although, it's not more difficult than other units I did before. I know this one is really not progressing."

"Why do you feel it is not progressing? What is blocking you? Do you need any help?" I asked.

"I don't exactly know. I redo different steps; some require more time. I am not sure I know the reason why." After a few seconds, John continued, "Somehow, I am not excited about this design."

"Do you find this design interesting? Are you excited to come to work and see what happens next?" I continued asking him.

"Not really. I feel work is just more of the same, and I am unable to innovate or express myself as before."

"If you really feel like that, maybe you should consider making a change," I suggested. Of course, for me to lose such a good and experienced engineer was a problem; but I thought that he would be happier if he found something he enjoys doing, and that I might get better results from someone who would enjoy his work and be excited about it.

After a few meetings, we found a new direction for him; and I got a new designer who took over his unit design. It was a win-win situation for everyone. Both designers were more motivated and excited about their roles and results, and the business got better results, with people enjoying their work.

I use these three principles with all my groups and organizations, and they have become an integral part of our organizational culture. My experiences through the years have helped me define these principles: I saw what was important, what was engaging people, what was driving business results and creating a positive and good working environment. I learned that these principles are very useful with different groups, different tasks and different cultures.

When I start working with a new organization, I present these principles to the entire team, and openly share with them my thoughts and point of view; I make these principles a part of the organizational culture. With the managers, I emphasize and explain even further, as I expect them to drive and follow these principles with their groups. This open sharing is important as it enables the team to get to know me faster and to know what to expect and what is important, and how I'll be leading the team. Showing my openness and, at the same time, helping them work better is an important, additional means of helping to engage and motivate the team.

Insights and Applications

- Three leadership principles:
  1. People are the most important asset. It is important to show this in actions and not just in words.
  2. Results mean Quality On Schedule.
  3. Enjoy the work—you will be more successful and so will the business.
- Share these principles openly in your organization. This will show your openness and drive people to be more engaged, caring and motivated.

ENDING

LEAVING A MARK

Long-Term Relationships

Leaving Intel, I went to the different offices I had worked in to thank my former employees and to say goodbye. Among the places I went to, one was Oregon, in the United States, where I had worked for four years. I was then managing a group of 25 employees there, called LOC. They had been designing one of the most complex functional units of the CPU, the new generation (at the time, it was the newest). The group started out small and grew over time, in view of the unit's complexity. This was my first relocation role in the States. Apart from the farewell gathering at Intel, in Oregon, I had a special meeting with my former group, LOC, that I had managed eighteen years before. When I had been offered my first relocation role, I had deliberated about whether to go, and I had had plenty of doubts. Eventually, I had decided to go, only after I made sure I could return at any time if I were not happy. This role was so good for me, I stayed there for four years. I was the manager of a group of about 25 people, and all through the years, we kept in close touch. Every time I visited Oregon, we met for dinner at a restaurant, and everyone showed up—even people who had transferred to other groups or had left the company. They all lived in Oregon in the same city, and they all got together only when I came for a visit. During these gatherings, the atmosphere was always positive and fun. Someone said he had transferred to another group and described how it was to work with people you did not know. Another shared about her daughter, who plays the piano and who took on skiing—despite her mother's displeasure with this hobby. We recalled how one of the architects had proposed a change and had promised that it would be easy, even though we understood that this change was highly complex—and eventually, the change was found indeed to be complex and took time to realize. We also recalled the moment, as we were approaching the end of the project but I had to return to Israel, that they'd decided to give me a trophy, even though I was not able to finish the project with them. We recalled stressful times and shared successes. Maintaining such a relationship for eighteen years is extraordinary. For me, it is extremely rewarding and empowering, and generates the enthusiasm required to continue, to invest, to work from the soul—caring for other people and creating working relationships with special connections.

In retrospect, when looking at how this unique connection formed, everything happened out of small, everyday actions that demonstrated caring, mutual help and true sharing. When I had just started working in the States, I used to go through the cubicles every morning and greet everyone, checking how they were. At first, everybody found it strange; but soon, it became a habit, and most people told me news about themselves, what they had done over the weekend, which good movie they had seen—or they simply "small-talked." Everybody had said that Shlomit's corridor was the loudest. Most Americans are quiet and don't speak in corridors, and our habit became the group joke—our being loud. This was a small act that brought about the formation of the group as it is.

For instance, one weekend, we threw a families' picnic. I was told of a nice green park, and I was thrilled to hold the picnic there. Everyone was enthusiastic and organized what we would eat, who would collect the money, who would shop for food, who would bring activities or music. The enthusiasm of the preparations was great, and it became the talk of the day until the weekend we met in the park. For my team, it was the first time that their families had gotten together (even though some people had been working together for a few years prior); it was very successful. We met their spouses and children, and some even brought their grandparents; we got to know one another's hobbies; we played, laughed and enjoyed a good and fun atmosphere. Such an event empowers the team, enables a different type of acquaintance – unrelated to work – and opens up new aspects of familiarity and sharing.

The bonds formed in the group not only were social but also

were characterized by true help and support at work. Once a week, we held team meetings, and – to encourage active participation and not only listening – I started a custom by which each person had to tell their greatest success of the week, and the greatest difficulty or problem they were currently dealing with. At first, the sharing felt coerced; they barely found things to share about, and it appeared as if they were only talking to me and that I was the only one connecting all the dots. I asked who could help them with their problem; I explained how one person's success could help another person in his next task. I gave them shared assignments if they came across similar problems. Since I knew and understood the tasks of the entire group, I could help and direct them to cooperate at work and to help one another. With time, they started to show a growing interest in one another's assignments, and my role as mediator was less needed. In one of the meetings, we had a few urgent matters, and I neglected the "updates round" from the group. When they learned that the meeting was over, they reminded me that we had not had the updates today, and that they could stay a little longer, just if we could go over everybody's updates. I felt that they were missing it; and it became a regular part of their work. Something additional that helped creating a special bond was our common debugging. Sometimes, our shared work was when we sat at the computer to solve problems spontaneously. Someone would complain about something he was stuck with, and immediately, two or three others came around his desk and tried out different solutions together. During stressful periods, we stayed late to help one another out and to send a better prepared unit.

A collection of small deeds had led to the formation of the group, to true caring for one another, to friendship and to a special atmosphere. This was the reason that, even after eighteen years, everybody found the time and enjoyed getting together.

"Mice" Mementos

One day, just as I was writing these lines, I received a text message from an unknown number with a picture of a computer mouse with a dedication, which I had given as a present to an organization I had been a manager in for ten years. I had left that organization five years before, and as a farewell gift, every employee (there were more than 1,000 employees) had received a computer mouse with the dedication: "To my Outstanding Team. Thank You, Shlomit"

I had personally handed the gift to each employee, and they had thanked me and marveled; it is not every day that a manager who leaves hands out mementos to his employees. After so many years, it was obvious to me that the mice don't exist anymore, and that no one even remembers them. It sometimes amazes me how much people recall of us—even things that we have forgotten. But the image he sent me that day was surprising, and it was followed with correspondence:

Zvika (by the name, I recognized that it was one of the leading employees in the Jerusalem group): "Would you believe it?"

Me: "I wouldn't believe it if I didn't see it. There are still people who remember where this came from?"

Zvika: "Certainly! And I will surprise you; you are remembered for the best—especially here in Jerusalem. I have three mice because of people who left. I asked them to give the mice to me so I can give them to someone new. The new people ask about the story of these mice, and we tell them."

Me: "Thank you; that is so nice to hear. It is exciting to be remembered and paid forward. Thank you for sharing."

This was a special experience for me, and it shows, without a doubt, the influence I had on people's lives, and that they remember and follow my lead.

The Jerusalem group has a special story. It was integrated with the large design group I had managed since about six years before. In view of the cancelation of a project and a whole area they were working in, it was decided to transfer them to CPU design. They rather objected the transfer. They did not want to transfer, nor did they want to be a part of a larger group. The group manager was not supportive of the transfer and made the change even more difficult.

When I understood the situation, at first, I talked to the manager and tried to coax him and make him cooperate. Unfortunately, he kept resisting and constantly found reasons why what was done to the group was wrong. After a few conversations, I gave him two options: He could either accept the change and make it into a success, or if he felt he did not want or could not do it, he could transfer to another role. I was clear; a manager cannot be in a state where he is constantly resisting and explaining why things are not good or are not going to work. After a few talks, he chose to move on and search for a new role. I knew the group was really attached to him and that his employees would take it hard, so I went in person to tell them about this change.

At first, I met his staff and explained to them my point of view: "I believe people should enjoy their work, at least most of the time. They should come to work willingly and full of motivation, to do their best for themselves and for the company. It is especially important for managers, as they lead others to follow them and to generate a team atmosphere. A manager can create an atmosphere of excellence only if he enjoys himself and if he is motivated." Everyone agreed silently with the general tone but did not see where I was going. I carried on: "Unfortunately, after a few talks I held with Shalom, he decided that CPU does not interest him, and he does not believe he will enjoy this role. He chose to move on to another group. I know you all were attached to him, but I believe that you understand that this is the right thing for him and for this group. I trust you, as management, to maintain this group and its qualities, and to help others make the shift and to succeed in their new direction. I truly hope that you are excited with this change, see the many opportunities and are energized for success. If there is anyone who does not think or feel this way, I would be happy if he comes to talk to me." The room fell silent. Everyone was shocked by the announcement I had made and the clear message I had sent through it, that I expect complete cooperation and want people to enjoy what they are doing. I wrapped up the meeting, and some managers came and asked how to break the news to the team. I said I would hold a meeting with the team and let them know. It was important to provide a unified message to everyone, to explain the circumstances and to create motivation and expectations for interesting work and successes to come.

After about two hours, I gathered the entire Jerusalem team and notified them about the change: "I am thrilled you are joining the CPU design team, and I am confident this is an important opportunity for you, one that allows you to cooperate more and face a very interesting challenge—the CPU. I believe that people should enjoy their work and find interest in it, and I hope this is the situation for you. Unfortunately, at this stage, Shalom decided that this is not the way he wants to go; and therefore, we decided, together, that he should transfer to another role, in another team." I paused; the room was intensely silent. People were looking at one another and at me, trying to figure things out; did this mean anything about them? Who would take Shalom's place? What would the organization look like? I continued: "The entire management team is staying and everyone shall maintain their positions. Together, we shall redefine the right management for the entire group. In the meantime, all tasks will continue, and everybody fits their new roles in the CPU group." Continuity was an important value for me to guarantee; it was important I show that things were clear and stable and to avoid providing a feeling of crisis and uncertainty.

"Good luck, everyone; I am confident we will continue together, as a team, and succeed in everything. If there are any questions or comments, you can come talk to me. I am here for the day."

The meeting was adjourned; small groups of people gathered and tried to guess the future – who would manage the group, what it would be like – until they slowly went back to work. That entire day, I sat in the Jerusalem cafeteria, making myself available for my employees. A few of them came to me, wondering what would happen with Shalom and where he was going. I promised everyone we were looking for an opportunity that would be good for him, in which he would enjoy himself and would be satisfied.

In a short while, everyone went back to work; Shalom moved to another team; and his managers did an excellent job preserving the organization and the people, continuing to provide good results, as expected.

This was my first contact with the Jerusalem group. It was not simple—I had had to give them a message they never wanted to receive; it is difficult to part with a manager. The direct and open conversation helped them figure out that I was looking out for the best interests of the group, that it was important for me that things work out and that I wanted them to be well-integrated in the organization.

Later, this group had many differences of opinion about work methods and methodologies, and these involved many arguments with other parts of the organization. I was involved in big decisions when they couldn't reach a consensus. Each party held strongly to its side. I always made sure to be very transparent with my considerations; I always asked that each side would consider the pros and cons of the method it offered. If someone saw only pros, I sent him to do additional research. We held a pros-and-cons conversation with everyone and tried to figure out objections. In my decisions, I always make sure to be clear and direct, to explain the criteria and to ensure they understand the direction I was going in and why I was going there. They did not always like the answer; sometimes they felt they were "losing" to other parts of the organization, but they always received a clear and direct explanation regarding the reason for the decision and its meaning.

With time, the group was accepted as a genuine part of the organization, and we bonded thanks to my openness in our talks and the ability to tell the truth like it is. This openness allowed them to understand the decisions, accept them and make peace with the work methods. They maintained contact and customs, through the computer "mouse," the gift I had left behind.

Leaving a Mark

I believe that my influence and my results were achieved thanks to my management and leadership style and methods; I gave everything from the bottom of my heart; I showed every person how much I care; I respected everyone and, even in stressful situations, I supported and guided my employees to do the right thing. At the same time, I always set a high standard with demands for high-quality results, on time and without compromise. In this book, I presented many examples of working from the bottom of your heart and soul, and of the special treatment that makes people communicate, devote themselves and be caring. It is well known in the professional literature that caring for every employee is the most important and influential factor to the success of the group and the entire company. To achieve maximized success, and to receive the personal gratification of success and influence, it is important to work with your heart and soul—but without giving up on professionalism, without giving up on the effort required to perform tasks, without giving up on results and quality. Therefore, it was important to me to manage engineering alongside people, and to manage people alongside engineering and to understand the mutual dependency between the two fields. What happens with people when projects are delayed—canceled? Mediocracy starts? And what happens with engineering when hearts are invisible, dissatisfied and unexcited? Engineering and people, tasks and individuals—all these must go hand in hand.

This concept includes many opposing elements, such as:

Managing professionally under stress, without compromise, while being caring and supportive; leadership; vision; professionalism; values and an honest concern for people; attentiveness; real sharing and much more.

The ability to include opposing leadership practices is one of the most significant tools that I implement. It promotes exceptional success and excellence over time. Contradictions exist and they are human – there is no reason to hide them – and the more we manage them together correctly, we will be authentic leaders, we will be able to engage our employees and our employees will trust us.

There are plenty of good leaders, but an excellent leader is one that is remembered and whose methods are continued. I believe that it is possible to be a great leader and leave a mark through the right balance of managing contradictions, having a benevolent and respectful attitude in any situation—even the most stressful ones. The mark you leave behind is the way to know all your hard work paid off.

I will finish with the words of Nat King Cole:

"Unforgettable, that's what you are.
Unforgettable, though near or far."